Getting To Know...

Nature's Children

PRONGHORNS

Elma Schemenauer

GROLIER
BOOKS

Facts in Brief

Classification of the Pronghorn

      Class: *Mammalia* (mammals)

      Order: *Artiodactyla* (cloven-hoofed mammals)

      Family: *antilocapridae*

      Genus: *antilocapra*

      Species: *antilocapra americana*

World distribution. Exclusive to North America.

Habitat. Open country: plains, deserts, foothills.

Distinctive physical characteristics. Black branched or "pronged" horns with curved tips; short black-tipped mane; tan coat with white throat and rump.

Habits. Active during the day; high-spirited; lives in herds.

Diet. Weeds, grasses, shrubs.

Edited by: Elizabeth Grace Zuraw
Design/Photo Editor: Nancy Norton
Photo Rights: Ivy Images

ISBN: 0-7172-8842-0

Have you ever wondered . . .

You may know these song words—

Home, home on the range,

Where the deer and the antelope play...

And if you've seen a TV show about America's western plains, you may have seen a pronghorn—or antelope, as the song calls it—bounding across the wide, open spaces.

The Blackfoot Indians of the western plains told this story about the pronghorn: Long ago the Old Man (God) was in the mountains. He took some earth and made a pronghorn, then let it loose. The pronghorn bounded up a steep slope, but there were many rocks in the mountains. The poor pronghorn fell and hurt itself.

Seeing that the mountains weren't right for the pronghorn, the Old Man sent the animal down to the plains. There the pronghorn ran like the wind. It looked so happy streaking gracefully across the windswept plains that the Old Man knew that was just the right spot for it!

This Native American legend may not be actual fact, but it does tell a basic truth about the pronghorn: With its great bounding leaps, this elegant and spirited animal is a thrilling sight, indeed.

Playful Pronghorns

Opposite page: *A newborn pronghorn can run fast, but it can't keep up a high speed for long distances. When danger appears, the baby hides in the grass.*

Even as babies, pronghorns are good runners. By the second day of life, these newborns have already taught themselves to run— though they're still a bit shaky on their feet. If you were to race a two-day-old pronghorn, you'd probably still beat it.

The next day, however, you wouldn't have a chance. The baby pronghorn would already be running too fast for you. And by its seventh day, it would run faster than most dogs and horses!

No wonder young pronghorns love running games. They prance around and around in circles. They chase each other as if playing tag. They even run group races. Several youngsters will speed away, swing around in a big circle, and then race back to their waiting mothers.

Pronghorn mothers often lie down to rest. Sometimes, just for fun, the baby pronghorns jump from one resting mother's back onto another mother's back. How do you think the mothers like such bouncing babies?

A Small Family

Like deer, goats, and cattle, pronghorns are *herbivores,* animals that eat plants. And like these animals, they also have split *hoofs,* or feet. You may think a pronghorn looks some-what like a small deer, but it isn't closely related to deer. For that matter, it isn't closely related to goats or cattle either. In fact, prong-horns have no close relatives anywhere in the world. They belong to a family all their own.

Early explorers thought pronghorns were antelope, and some people still incorrectly call them by that name. Other people call them pronghorn antelope. Pronghorns, however, are not related to the antelope of Africa and Asia, and the correct name for this animal really is just simply pronghorn.

Facial and chest markings on the pronghorn vary from animal to animal.

Home on the Range

Opposite page:

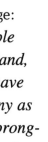

Before people settled the land, there may have been as many as 35 million pronghorns in North America. Today there are fewer than a million.

Pronghorns are found only on the plains of North America. In the United States, most pronghorns live on the western rangelands of Wyoming and Montana. Occasionally some can be found roaming the plains from Iowa west to the mountains along the Pacific Coast. In Mexico, pronghorns live in the central regions of the country. And in Canada, they live on the sagebrush-dotted prairies of southern Alberta and Saskatchewan. A *prairie* is a flat treeless area where grasses grow.

When explorers first came to North America, there were huge herds of pronghorns all over the western plains. Today, however, it isn't so easy to see them. Now these animals live only in the most deserted parts of the great plains, far from people, fences, and buildings. And since pronghorns are nervous creatures, they don't live long when kept as zoo animals or pets. It seems they need the freedom of the open range.

The shaded area on this map shows where pronghorns live.

Prairie Speedsters

Pronghorns love to run. They even like racing with moving objects.

Opposite page:
When pronghorns run, they can leap across a distance of up to 25 feet (7.6 meters) in one bound!

People who drive cars through pronghorn country sometimes are treated to a pleasant surprise. A group of pronghorns may suddenly appear from behind a low hill and start running alongside the car. Faster and faster the animals bound along, trying to stay ahead of the vehicle.

All at once, the animals will put on a burst of speed. Then they'll cut across the road *in front* of the car!

Once the pronghorns have crossed the road, they seem to feel the race is over. They stop and stare at the car and driver, looking quite pleased with themselves.

Pronghorns have been clocked at speeds as great as 60 miles (95 kilometers) per hour. Some people believe that the pronghorn is one of the fastest animals on Earth—second only to the cheetah.

Born To Run

A close look at a grown-up pronghorn shows that this animal is built to run. The pronghorn has very large hoofs for the size of its body. These hoofs have firm, yet bouncy, pads underneath that help to keep the animal's feet from getting sore as it pounds across the plains. The pronghorn also has strong, well-developed muscles in its slim legs.

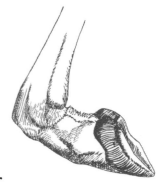

Pronghorn hoof

Surprisingly, the pronghorn's body is rather chunky. A full-grown pronghorn stands about 3 feet (1 meter) tall at the shoulder. It weighs about 100 pounds (45 kilograms).

You might not think that such a chunky body would be good for running fast, but it is. Inside its wide chest, the pronghorn has a super-sized windpipe, large lungs to hold a lot of air, and a huge heart. The pronghorn's heart, for instance, is twice as big as a sheep's heart, yet the two animals weigh about the same.

Pronghorns often seem to run just for the sheer fun of it.

Keeping Up the Pace

Have you ever run hard and then had to stop because you were out of breath and your muscles hurt too much to keep going? It takes a long time for this to happen to a pronghorn. That's because its body is built to take in lots of *oxygen,* the part of the air we breathe that is used by the body. And a pronghorn's body also quickly carries away the wastes (such as lactic acid) that make the muscles ache. Such a well-equipped body allows this prairie speedster to run fast over long distances. The pronghorn's endurance makes it a long-distance champ.

Female pronghorns, called *does,* can run faster than *bucks,* as the males are called. A playful doe may tease a buck by getting him to run after her. Often she leads him on a long and merry chase.

Gathering together is one way pronghorns have of defending themselves against enemies. And often when pronghorns are in a group, each animal faces in a different direction to keep a better lookout.

A Coat That Blends In

The pronghorn's coat is a gray, tan, or reddish-brown color, just like the sun-baked prairie earth. Its cheeks, throat, belly, and rump are white. Smart-looking black markings trim its face and throat.

This "blend-in" color scheme, which is called *camouflage,* makes the pronghorn hard to see from far away. When standing still, this animal almost disappears among the brownish shrubs and grass of the dry plains. Camouflage helps protect the pronghorn from *predators,* animals that hunt other animals for food.

Close up, you can clearly see this pronghorn. But across a distance, its camouflage would make this animal hard to spot.

All-weather Coats

The pronghorn's coarse, hairy coat keeps this animal comfortable in all kinds of weather. The coat actually is two coats in one. Long *guard hairs* that make up the coat's outer layer keep out rain and snow. Short inner fur that's close to the animal's skin keeps out the cold.

When the hot sun bakes the prairie, the pronghorn uses special muscles to make its guard hairs stand up straight. This allows cool breezes to pass through the animal's fur. Then when cold winter winds howl across the prairie, the pronghorn uses those same muscles to flatten its guard hairs. The hairs then overlap to form a cozy "blanket."

You probably have different coats for winter and spring. So does the pronghorn. In late fall, it grows a thick, warm winter coat. In spring, it *molts,* or sheds the coat. A shedding pronghorn can look pretty untidy, with thick folds of old fur hanging from its sides.

A molting pronghorn is a messy-looking pronghorn.

Special Headgear

The pronghorn gets its name from its *pronged,* or branched, horns. Each horn has one prong.

The headgear of the pronghorn is different from that of any other animal in the world. Deer, elk, and moose grow *antlers*—solid, bony, branched growths that the animals shed every year. Pronghorns, on the other hand, don't grow antlers. They grow true horns that are like the horns of cattle, sheep, and goats. The horns are hard, *hollow* covers over bony cores. They are *not* solid bony growths like antlers.

Every fall the pronghorns shed their hollow horn covers. The bony cores, which are covered with special hairs, are all that remain. These hairs are the beginnings of new horn covers that will take seven to eight months to reach their full growth. Pronghorns are the only animals in the world that shed their horn covers every year.

Opposite page: The horns of male pronghorns, can be quite long— about 15 inches (38 centimeters). Females usually have much smaller horns or, sometimes, none at all.

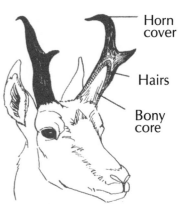

Horn cover

Hairs

Bony core

Cutaway of a pronghorn's horn.

All the Better To See You With

Pronghorns have huge, jet-black eyes and excellent vision. Their eyes are even bigger than those of a horse, which is a much larger animal than a pronghorn.

A man once told of looking for pronghorns through a strong pair of binoculars. He spied a buck on a ridge almost 1 mile (1.5 kilometers) away. To his surprise, the man saw that the buck was staring right back at him!

The pronghorn could see just as well as the man using binoculars—in fact, probably better. Many people believe that pronghorns can see about eight times farther than a human can. Such sharp eyesight is important for animals that live on the vast treeless prairie where there are few places to hide. These animals need to be able to see predators from far off in order to avoid them. A *predator* is an animal that hunts other animals for food. A pronghorn's keen vision is its key defense. Because of it, sneaking up on a pronghorn is pretty much impossible.

The Watchful Eye

Pronghorns are noted for their curiosity and seem to enjoy observing the behavior of other animals. Sometimes they trail along behind a coyote simply to watch it hunt mice and other small animals. Of course, the coyote probably isn't very pleased to have such an uninvited audience tagging along!

Road builders have told remarkable stories about the inquisitive pronghorn. Workers have seen these animals stand on a ridge for hours on end, watching the men and their machines at work. But at any sign of danger, these shy, nervous creatures turn and quickly speed away.

Pronghorns' curiosity is easily aroused, but these animals do their watching from a safe distance.

Buttercups for Breakfast

Pronghorns are dainty, careful eaters. They nibble a few leaves and flowers here…some twigs there…a bit of bark somewhere else. Their favorite summer foods are clover, alfalfa, buttercups, and wild onions. In spring, they find fresh grass shoots especially tasty. In winter, they paw through snow to find plants and shrubs such as sagebrush.

Pronghorns do little harm to the prairie landscape as they eat. They step carefully so they don't trample plants they're not eating. This means they leave behind few signs to show where they've been feeding.

Like a deer or cow, when a pronghorn eats, it collects unchewed food, called *cud,* in a special part of its stomach. Later it lies down to rest and brings the cud back up to its mouth for chewing.

Though it may feed at any time of the day, a pronghorn is most active during the early morning and late afternoon.

In winter, pronghorns try to avoid deep snow.
If they had to paw for their food through heavy
snow, they'd use up a lot of energy that would
otherwise help keep them warm.

Finding Food in Winter

If there's enough food in an area, pronghorns may spend months there, even though the area may be no larger than 2 square miles (5 square kilometers). Pronghorns aren't great travelers. This may be partly because roads, fences, and train tracks now divide up much of their home range. Since pronghorns can't jump very high, even though they can jump long distances, they avoid leaping over fences. As a result, it's more difficult for them to travel far, though they have developed the skill of climbing *under* and *through* fences with surprising speed.

When winter arrives, however, pronghorns head for sheltered valleys. There it takes longer for snow to cover the ground, so food is easier to find. As winter progresses and the snow begins to deepen in the valleys, pronghorns head for steep, windswept hillsides where the snow tends to be blown away. There the pronghorns are more likely to find places with the most food and the least snow.

Mating Dance

In late summer, a pronghorn buck begins to behave oddly. With eyes bulging, the buck lowers his head and waves it from side to side. Then he quickly jumps to the left and the right, while ruffling his rump fur in wave-like motions. What's going on?

It's *mating season,* the time of year during which animals come together to produce young. The buck's behavior is his way of attracting females.

A pronghorn buck usually gathers a *harem,* or group of up to 25 does. Until mating season is over, he'll chase away any other buck that tries to approach the females in his harem.

Only the strongest, fastest, and most aggressive bucks get the chance to mate. All the other bucks aren't strong enough or experienced enough to fight off the few most powerful, superior bucks.

A pronghorn buck tries to impress a group of does.

Springtime Babies

By the time spring arrives, the pronghorn doe is ready to give birth.

Unlike many animal mothers, a pronghorn mother doesn't make a den or prepare a nursery nest. Instead, when she's about to give birth she looks for a secluded place away from the herd. Often she chooses a spot that has lots of tall plants around it so that she and her babies won't be seen. There she usually has twins, though sometimes she may have one or even three babies.

A doe is ready to start a family before she's two years old. Bucks mature about the same time but they don't mate until they're about five years old. It takes males that long to determine who is the strongest among them.

A doe seeks privacy when she is about to give birth.

My, What Big Eyes You Have

A baby pronghorn, or *fawn,* seems to be all eyes, ears, and legs. Its eyes and ears look too big for its narrow face, and its "toothpick" legs seem much too long for its bony little body!

You may be surprised to learn that a baby pronghorn and a human baby weigh more or less the same at birth. Normally, a newborn pronghorn weighs from 6 to 8 pounds (2.7 to 3.6 kilograms). Weights do vary, however. Some pronghorn fawns weigh as little as 2.2 pounds (1 kilogram).

As soon as the fawns are born, the mother pronghorn cleans them by licking them all over. This also removes any of her scent that may linger on them. Since very young fawns have almost no scent of their own, predators such as coyotes, bobcats, Golden Eagles, or foxes are unable to sniff them out—and then make a meal of them.

Within about 15 minutes of birth, a baby pronghorn is standing and walking.

Lying Low

For the first week or so of its life, a baby prong-horn spends most of its time alone in its own special hiding place, called a *cache* (pronounced CASH). The cache is any convenient spot that's hidden among tall weeds or bushes. There the newborn lies flat on the ground, completely out of view.

A pronghorn mother doesn't stay too close to her babies because her scent might attract predators. Instead, she finds a spot a short distance away. From there she keeps a close watch on her babies' hiding places.

At this age, the fawns *nurse,* or drink milk from their mother's body. Because the milk is the fawns' only nourishment, their mother visits the babies several times a day. But before she does, she carefully looks around to make sure there's no danger nearby. If a predator comes too close to a fawns' cache, the mother tries to lead the intruder away. If this doesn't work, she fights, kicking hard with her sharp hoofs. Usually a determined pronghorn mother can drive away a hungry coyote or bobcat.

Opposite page:
A baby pronghorn hides in its cache. Fawns have coats of dappled gray— good camouflage to protect them from enemies.

Joining a Band

A baby pronghorn remains cached for about three weeks. However, when it's safe, the baby starts coming out after about a week to join in the activities of its mother's *band,* or group. Usually this band is made up of one buck, several does, and several fawns.

When the young pronghorns join the band, they start playing with the other fawns. What a good time they have, running and jumping and butting heads. But all this activity is more than just fun for a little pronghorn. By running, jumping, and chasing, it builds up its muscles and endurance. The more it plays, the stronger and more agile it becomes.

A pronghorn mother enjoys romping with her babies, but she's always on the alert for any signs of danger.

Baby-sitting Services

Sometimes pronghorn mothers want to get away for a while from all the activity of their lively offspring. How do they manage to take a break? They leave one doe in charge of the fawns while the rest of them go off to feed or rest. This pronghorn baby-sitting system works quite well. Often one doe will be left to watch 10 or 12 fawns at a time. When their mothers return, the fawns run to them, eager for a drink of warm milk.

Baby pronghorns don't live just on milk for long. Between the ages of three to six weeks, they begin to eat tender green leaves and young shoots.

By the age of three months, this fawn will have acquired a fur coat similar to that of its parents.

Warning Signals

Danger! When a pronghorn senses a predator nearby, it often snorts a warning to other pronghorns. But this animal also has another way of sending danger signals. It can tighten its skin muscles to lift the long hairs of the large white patch on its rump. This raised white patch flashes a warning to other pronghorns that danger is near. It also signals those pronghorns to flare their rump hairs, too, as a warning to yet other pronghorns.

As soon as the pronghorns get the message, they gather in a group and run from the danger. Usually a doe leads the fleeing pronghorns. A large buck runs at the end of the line, acting as a sort of rear guard. If a coyote or other predator comes near him, the buck strikes at it with his sharp hoofs or butts it with his horns.

Pronghorns also use scent signals to warn each other of danger. A pronghorn has several scent glands on its body. A *gland* is a part of an animal's body that makes and gives out a substance. The pronghorn uses its scent glands to send out smells as warning messages.

Opposite page: Flared white rumps are a signal for pronghorns to flee from nearby danger. With their excellent eyesight, pronghorns can easily get the message—even across long distances.

Growing Up Fast

Baby pronghorns grow up quite quickly. By the age of four months, they begin to send scent signals and to flash their white rump hairs when danger arises. By fall, when they're about five or six months old, they've stopped nursing and are eating only plants— just like their parents.

The young pronghorns stay with the adult herd for the winter. Together they have a better chance of surviving the howling prairie blizzards and the long, cold nights.

When spring arrives, bringing sunshine and new, tender green shoots, the young prong- horns are a year old. By fall, the females will be old enough to mate.

If a young pronghorn is lucky, it will live to enjoy the freedom of its home on the range for eight or nine more years.

Words To Know

Antlers   Solid, bony, branched growths on an animal's head.

Band   A group of pronghorns.

Buck   A male pronghorn.

Cache   A hiding spot for a newborn pronghorn.

Camouflage   The coloring and markings on an animal that blend in with the animal's surroundings.

Cud   Hastily swallowed food brought back up for chewing by cud chewers such as cows, deer, and pronghorns.

Doe   A female pronghorn.

Fawn   A young pronghorn.

Gland   Part of an animal's body that makes and gives off a substance.

Guard hairs   Long coarse hairs that make up the outer layer of a pronghorn's coat.

Harem   A group of does that a buck mates with and protects from other bucks.

Herbivore   An animal that eats plants.

Hoofs   The feet of pronghorns, deer, cattle, and some other animals.

Horns   Head growths on a pronghorn that consist of hard hollow covers over bony cores.

Mate   To come together to produce young. Either member of an animal pair is also the other's mate.

Molt   To shed one coat of fur or feathers and to grow another.

Nurse   To drink milk from a mother's body.

Prairie   A flat treeless area where grasses grow.

Predator   An animal that hunts other animals for food.

Prong   A branch or thin, pointed object.

Index

PHOTO CREDITS
Cover: Esther Schmidt, *Valan Photos.* **Interiors:** *Valan Photos:* Wilf Schurig, 4, 25; Stephen J. Krasemann, 7, 42; Wayne Lankinen, 8, 11; Dennis Schmidt, 13, 14, 18, 22, 45; Esther Schmidt, 26, 33, 34, 38, 41; Don McPhee, 29. /Tim Fitzharris, 17, 21. /*Ivy Images:*Alan & Sandy Carey, 30, 37.

Getting To Know...

Nature's Children

SEALS

Merebeth Switzer

GROLIER
BOOKS

Facts in Brief

Classification of North American earless seals

    Class: *Mammalia* (mammals)

    Order: *Carnivora* (meat-eaters)

    Family: *Phocidae* (seal family)

    Genus and species: 13 genera and 18 species around the world; most common in North America: Harbor Seal, Harp Seal, Ringed Seal, Bearded Seal, Gray Seal, Hooded Seal, Northern Elephant Seal

World Distribution.   Seals are found throughout the Polar regions, and as far south as California and New York in North America, Wales in Europe, and Japan in Asia.

Habitat.   Usually live where ocean water meets land or solid ice; may move into fresh water; some migrate in search of food.

Distinctive Physical Characteristics.   Has no external ears, simply openings on side of head; rear flippers cannot be turned forward; coarse stiff coat with no underfur.

Diet.   Mainly fish but also various other sea animals.

Edited by: Elizabeth Grace Zuraw
Design/Photo Editor: Nancy Norton
Photo Rights: Ivy Images

ISBN: 0-7172-8843-9

Have you ever wondered . . .

What barks like a dog, has whiskers like a cat, and swims like a fish? If you guessed a seal, congratulations! Seals have an unusual combination of features that equip them for life on land as well as in the water. They're one of the few animals that are at home in both worlds.

When people think about seals, they often picture performing seals. But most of the animals that perform in zoos and marine parks are not seals, they're Sea Lions.

The seal, nonetheless, is a superb swimmer, and it can put on a flashy show of its own. It can perform a combination of spins, twirls, and somersaults, then disappear below the water's surface in an amazing speed dive.

On land, seals are not as graceful as they are in the water. But they seem to enjoy sunbathing and "talking" to friends, much as human vacationers do at a beach.

A Harbor Seal rests on a sandy shore. Harbor Seals stay close to home, seldom venturing more than 10 miles from where they were born.

Inquisitive Pups

The sleek, smooth body of a pudgy young seal skims through the water of a harbor. Suddenly the baby seal, called a *pup,* stops and pops its head up to check its surroundings. Its large brown eyes focus on a sailboat quietly gliding by. Overcome by curiosity, the pup watches while bobbing closer to the strange object. Then all at once, a huge flapping sail unfurls on the boat. The pup dives fast—and deep— into the water. Even though the young adventurer is curious, it'll leave *this* giant sea monster alone!

A young seal's playful curiosity disappears as it grows up and becomes more cautious about the world around it. Such watchfulness is important. In order to survive, the pup must learn to be wary of its surroundings.

Gray Seal pups are white at birth. As adults, Gray Seals vary in color from pale gray to nearly black. Females often are lighter than the males.

Fin-footed Families

There are many different kinds of seals. They all belong to a group of animals called *pinnipeds,* which means "fin-footed." You have only to look at these animals' large, flipper-like feet to know why scientists have given them this name. And flippers are very useful to a seal. When a creature spends as much time in the water as pinnipeds do, flippers are much more practical than ordinary feet.

Eared seal

The pinniped group is made up of three families—walruses, eared seals (which include Sea Lions and fur seals), and earless seals, often called true seals. The earless seal family is the biggest and most widespread of the three pinniped families. There are 18 kinds of earless seals and about half of them are found in North America.

Earless seal

A fur seal belongs to the eared seal family. In this photo, the small earflaps are clearly visible on either side of the seal's head.

Seal front flipper

Sea Lion front flipper

Seal or Sea Lion?

It's not surprising that people sometimes get seals and Sea Lions confused. But if you look closely, you'll notice some differences.

First look at the ears. Sea Lions have ears that are easy to see. They belong to the group of seals called eared seals. Although true seals have ears, too, their ears are only tiny openings on the sides of their heads. They don't have earflaps as Sea Lions do.

Both seals and Sea Lions are beautifully streamlined for life in the water, but their hind flippers are quite different. As a result, the two animals swim and move on land in different ways. Sea Lions can walk and even run on land because they can stand on their hind flippers. In the water they paddle with their large front flippers and steer with their back flippers. Seals use their hind flippers as a huge fin to do most of the swimming work.

On land, a seal's hind flippers are of little use. Instead of walking, a seal wiggles along like an overgrown caterpillar.

Creature of Two Worlds

The seal is a creature of two worlds—water and land. In water, it moves with grace and ease. And unlike most aquatic animals, it can move from salt water to fresh water if the need arises.

At the same time, the seal is a *mammal,* and one feature of a mammal is that it has lungs and it needs to breathe air. That need takes the seal ashore, where it also goes to rest and to *mate,* or produce young.

From the Arctic *ice floes*—large floating pieces of flat ice—to the rocky shores of Newfoundland and the sandy beaches of California, the seal lives in areas where water meets land and solid ice.

Opposite page: A baby Harp Seal is quite at home in its frozen world of ice and snow.

In North America, seals can be found as far south as New York on the Atlantic Coast, and all the way down to California and Mexico on the Pacific Coast.

Watery Wonder

A seal is wonderfully suited to its watery existence. Its sleek, torpedo-shaped body glides easily through the water and helps make the animal an excellent swimmer.

Seals are remarkable in their ability to remain underwater for long periods of time— 20 minutes or more. How do they manage?

Before a seal dives, it breathes out all the air in its lungs. That makes diving easier and safer because the intense pressure found in deep water doesn't affect a seal if it has no air in its lungs. But the seal's heart and brain, like yours, need *oxygen*—the part of the air that is used by the body. Like you, the seal can get oxygen only from air. Unlike you, however, all the oxygen the seal needs underwater is contained in its blood. Until the seal comes to the surface again to breathe, most of the oxygen in the seal's blood goes to its most important body organs—the heart and brain.

Seals are world-class swimmers.

Diving Champs

Scuba divers must really envy seals. Without special equipment, human divers can go to a depth of only 150 feet (45 meters). Diving any deeper is dangerous. But many seals can dive twice as deep as a human. And some of these diving champs, such as the Elephant Seal, can reach depths of about 1,000 feet (300 meters)!

Your heart beats about 72 times a minute. A seal's heart normally beats much faster, about 150 times per minute. But when the seal dives, its heart rate drops to 60 beats per minute. On very deep or long dives, its heartbeat may drop as low as 10 to 20 beats a minute. By having its heart pump blood much more slowly, the seal can make the supply of oxygen in its blood last longer.

When it comes up for air, a seal breathes through its nostrils. But when the seal dives, the nostrils close.

Big, Beautiful Brown Eyes

A seal's large brown eyes have special features to help the animal see underwater. Because it can be very dark deep down in the ocean, the *pupils,* or inner circles, of a seal's eyes open extra wide to let in more light. Out of the water in bright sunlight, the pupils shrink to a tiny slit.

If you've ever kept your eyes open while swimming in the ocean, then you know that salt water soon makes your eyes sting. Seals don't have this problem. They have an extra, transparent eyelid that they can pull over their eyes to protect them when underwater.

Finally, seals do a lot of crying—but not because they're sad! Seals can't control the tears that flow from their eyes. Just as your eyes water in order to wash away specks of dust, seals' tears flow freely to wash away anything that might irritate their eyes.

A baby Harp Seal is called a whitecoat. *But when it grows up, it'll have a gray coat and a dark pattern on its back shaped like a harp, a curved musical instrument. Can you guess how Harp Seals got their name?*

Sizing Up Seals

Most types of seals range from 3 to 6 feet (1 to 2 meters) in length, and weigh from 200 to 500 pounds (90 to 225 kilograms). But male Northern Elephant Seals can grow to more than 20 feet (6 meters) in length, and weigh as much as 8,000 pounds (3,600 kilograms). That's longer than most people's living rooms and heavier than two cars! In fact, the Elephant Seal is one of the largest creatures on Earth.

As is the case with many animals, the males, or *bulls,* are often much bigger than the females, or *cows.*

Take a look at the huge nose and massive size of this animal. It's not hard to see how the Elephant Seal got its name!

A Blanket of Blubber

Imagine hopping into a bathtub full of freezing water and blocks of ice. Brrr! You'd feel like a human icicle just seconds after you plunged in! Not so with seals. They can spend long periods of time swimming in water that's often part ice. How do seals manage this chilly feat? They're protected by *blubber,* a thick layer of body fat under their skin. A seal's blubber can be up to 6 inches (15 centimeters) thick. This bountiful blanket of blubber acts as insulation, keeping a seal's body heat in and the cold out.

Blubber also helps to smooth out the seal's body shape, making it even more streamlined for swimming. And because blubber is light, it helps keep the seal afloat. The seal doesn't need to work so hard when swimming.

A seal finds its blubber very useful in another way, too. When necessary, the seal can go for weeks without eating, drawing the energy it needs from the blubber stored on its body.

*From one-third to nearly one-half of an
adult seal's weight consists of blubber.*

Air-conditioning Flippers

Believe it or not, a seal is kept so warm by its layer of blubber that it sometimes gets over-heated! Since the seal can't take off its blubber blanket when it gets hot, the animal has come up with another way to cool off. It gets rid of extra heat through its flippers.

The seal's flippers aren't covered with blubber. Instead, they're crisscrossed with blood vessels, When a seal gets too warm, it can pump large amounts of blood through its flippers. There the blood is cooled by the surrounding air or water. The cooled blood then returns to the rest of the body and soon the seal's temperature goes back to normal.

Telltale Teeth

The teeth and claws of seals are made up of layers, like tree rings. A new layer is added every year. By counting the layers, scientists can tell a seal's age. Some seals live 25 years or more in the wild.

The seal's natural enemies include Polar Bears, Killer Whales, sharks, and occasionally, wolves. Young seals are particularly vulnerable, especially during their first weeks of life. A Golden Eagle, walrus, or other large predator considers a baby seal an easy meal. A *predator* is an animal that hunts other animals for food.

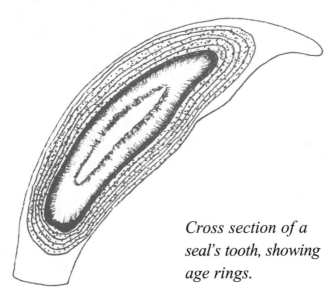

Cross section of a seal's tooth, showing age rings.

Who Are You?

To us, most seals look a lot alike. It's difficult to tell one from another. Seals seem to have the same problem we do. On a crowded beach they don't seem to be able—just by looking—to tell their own babies from other babies, or friends from strangers.

Instead, seals use smell and sound to help them identify one another. Most seals have a keen sense of smell. A mother seal uses it to recognize her own baby. This is very important if she's in a large group with other seals and their young.

Seals also use a wide range of calls to find a friend in a crowd. These "Who are you?" calls vary with the type of seal. Some seals make grunting and squeaking sounds, while others make dog-like barks.

Hooded Seals, found in the North Atlantic, are pale gray with black blotches and spots.

Seals—Together and Alone

When you think of seals, you may think of large groups of them clustered together on a beach. Or you may think of just a few seals playing together.

Many seals do live in groups. Some of them gather when they're ashore, but go their separate ways when they return to the water to feed. Others, such as the Harp Seal, spend all of their time in groups. During *mating season*—the time of year during which the seals come together to produce young—and while moving from one place to another, a group of Harp Seals may number in the thousands.

But there are other kinds of seals that prefer to live alone. The Ringed Seal, in particular, spends nearly all of its time on its own. The mother gives birth to one baby in a secluded *den,* or animal home, which she digs under snow or in a natural hollow in the ice. Mother and baby stay together for about two months. Except for this family-raising time, however, and a brief time spent with a partner during mating season, the Ringed Seal remains alone.

A herd of Harp Seals shares an icy realm. Social creatures, these seals prefer to live in groups rather than alone.

Seal-time Meal-time

Since seals search for food in the water, you can probably guess what one of their favorite foods is. That's right—fish.

But seals eat other foods as well. Harbor Seals search for small sea creatures in *tide pools,* patches of water left behind by the outgoing tide. The ocean-roaming Harp Seal eats small fish such as herring and capelin and masses of tiny, shrimp-like shellfish called *krill.*

Many seals prefer to eat bottom-living sea animals such as crabs, clams, whelks, shrimp, snails, and octopuses. In fact, a Bearded Seal has special whiskers like a walrus to help it search for tasty treats on the dark ocean bottom. Scientists think that the seal rakes up the bottom with its front claws and then uses its whiskers to sift through the debris. When the Bearded Seal finds a yummy whelk or succulent clam, it uses its strong jaws and teeth to crush the shell to get at the food. Since it doesn't need the shell in its diet, the seal spits out the broken pieces.

Opposite page: A seal's whiskers are sensitive feelers that help the animal find food in the murky ocean depths.

Long Journeys

You probably know that many birds *migrate*—they travel south every fall, then north again in the spring. But did you know that some seals do the same thing? When winter comes, seals that live in large groups in Arctic waters must migrate south to find food.

Harp Seals probably are the best known migrators. In summer, when northern waters teem with small fish and tiny sea animals, Harp Seals live and feed in the cold water at the edge of the Arctic's *pack ice*—the ice formed by the crashing together of chunks of ice. In the fall as the temperature goes down, the ice begins to spread southward over the seals' feeding grounds. The seals then have to move further south to stay ahead of the ice. Harp Seals migrate as much as 2,000 miles (3,200 kilometers) to their southern feeding grounds. When spring returns and the sun warms the air, the seals head north again, following the ice's melting edge.

Not all kinds of seals migrate. Those that live alone or in small groups don't make such long journeys.

Birth Time

Baby seals may be born at different times of the year, depending on which type of seal they are and where their home is. Most seal mothers, however, give birth in late winter. They haul themselves out onto the ice or onto land to have their babies.

Some cows gather in large groups to have their babies; others give birth alone. In either case, the bulls usually stay away from the females at this time. They may form bachelor groups or go off by themselves. They don't help care for the babies after they're born.

Where there's a seal pup this young, the mother probably isn't far away.

Meet the Baby

Seal babies are quite small compared to their mothers. Ringed Seal babies may weigh as little as 10 pounds (4.5 kilograms), while Bearded Seal pups may weigh as much as 80 pounds (36 kilograms.)

Most seals that are born on ice or snow have a soft, woolly white coat. A baby's coat is very important because it will keep the newcomer warm until its body has a chance to build up a layer of blubber. A white coat also helps the pup blend into its snowy home so that it's not easily spotted by predators.

Seals that are born on cliffs or sandy beaches are usually a dark brown or mottled color that matches their surroundings. Such a matching of colors, called *camouflage,* helps to hide and protect the young seals on the rocky or sandy beaches where they spend the first weeks of their life.

A Harbor Seal pup is usually born with a spotted coat very much like its mother's, except a little lighter in color.

A Caring Mother

A baby seal begins to *nurse,* or drink milk from its mother's body, minutes after it is born. Some babies nurse in the water; others do so on land or on ice floes. A mother seal's milk is so thick and rich that it looks like soft creamy butter.

A baby seal doesn't spend a long time with its mother, but while it is with her, it's well cared for. A mother seal stays near her baby, ready for its almost constant demands to nurse. If she does leave for any reason, she's seldom gone long.

Female Harbor Seals are ready to start a family when they're four years old. Males mature at five years of age.

Swimming Lessons

Seals are natural swimmers, but this doesn't mean that a baby seal jumps right into the water. This strange new wetness requires a close checking out before the first plunge is taken. The curious pup creeps up to the water's edge, and after a sniff and a sidelong glance, it plops itself into the water. There the flustered baby bobs about, unsure of its new surroundings. Soon, though, it'll be swimming with the same ease and grace as its mother. When it needs a rest, a tired pup may hitch a ride on its mother's shoulders.

Hooded Seal pups are called bluebacks *because of their blue-tinged fur.*

A Hasty Departure

Opposite page:
A male Hooded Seal inflates the stretchy skin over its nose into a large "hood." That's meant to warn intruders to stay away.

Some pups have two months or more of their mother's care, but many are left to fend for themselves when they're only about two weeks old. Still, these pups are well prepared for life on their own. They're already at home in the water, and most have grown-up teeth for feeding. In other words, they have all the tools they need to survive. They simply need to learn how to use them. And until they do learn to catch their own food, they can live off the blubber on their bodies.

There are reasons for the mother seal's rather hasty departure. If she is to have another baby the next year, she needs to seek out a male partner with whom she can mate. Also, the seal cow hasn't eaten since giving birth. In supplying milk for her baby, she has used up a great deal of her body fat. If she's to survive, mate, and have another baby, she must soon stop nursing her youngster.

Mating Time

Mating usually takes place a few weeks after the cows have left their pups. At this time the cows and bulls actively seek out each other. Some bulls put on spectacular swimming displays to impress a female, and often two bulls will fight each other to determine who will father the young.

Among some types of seals, a powerful bull may gather a *harem,* or group of several cows. He'll mate with the cows in his harem and protect them from the advances of other males. At first he'll probably just try to discourage an intruding male by lowering his head and hissing. If that doesn't work, he'll fight. Usually the intruder gives up and leaves before anyone is seriously hurt.

During mating season, some male seals give off a powerful musky odor. As unappealing as this smell may be to a human nose, it works just fine to attract female seals.

Opposite page: *Within two to three weeks of birth, a Gray Seal pup sheds its coat of creamy-white fur. The coat is replaced by a much darker one, similar to that of its parents.*

New Coats for Old

After adult seals mate, they *molt,* or shed their coats. By this time their old coats are ragged and shaggy. They've been worn away in many spots over the last year. In some cases, the coats shed in large pieces, sometimes taking old, dead outer skin with them.

While they're molting, seals rest and remain on land. They don't eat. Instead, they live off their stores of blubber. But within a few weeks, the bulls and cows have grown new coats of coarse fur.

It's now time to return to the ocean for their first meal in a long time. The seals eagerly head out in search of food. Most of the seals will live out in the ocean until the next spring when they'll again haul themselves out onto the land or ice where the next generation of pups will be born.

Seals have a fairly long life span—if they can overcome the risks they face both in the water and on land. Eared seals live to about 18 years of age. Earless seals live about 25 years.

Words To Know

Blubber   Layer of fat on an animal's body that keeps body heat in.

Bull   A male seal.

Camouflage   Animal features that blend in with its surroundings.

Cow   A female seal.

Den   An animal home.

Harem   A group of females that a bull mates with and protects.

Ice floes   Large floating pieces of flat ice.

Krill   Tiny, shrimp-like shellfish.

Lungs   The organ of the body that takes oxygen from the air and makes it available to the rest of the body.

Mammal   An animal that breathes air, is warm-blooded, is born live, drinks its mother's milk, and has some kind of hair during some stage of its life.

Mate   To come together to produce young.

Migration   Traveling at regular times of the year in search of food, a suitable climate, or a place to mate and raise young.

Molt   To shed a coat of fur or feathers and to grow another.

Nurse   To drink milk from a mother's body.

Oxygen   The part of the air we breathe that is used by the body.

Pack ice   Ice formed by the crashing together of chunks of ice.

Pinnipeds   A group of animals with feet specially shaped as flippers. Seals, Sea Lions, and walruses are pinnipeds.

Predator   An animal that hunts other animals for food.

Pup   A young seal.

Pupil   The part of the eye that opens and closes to take in light.

Tide pool   A pool of water left on shore when the tide goes out.

Index

PHOTO CREDITS
Cover: Kennon Cooke, *Valan Photos.* **Interiors:** *Valan Photos:* Harold V. Green, 4; Val & Alan Wilkinson, 7, 34; Stephen J. Krasemann, 8, 37; François Lepine, 16; W. Hoek, 26; Esther Schmidt, 30; Valan Photos, 40; Anthony J. Bond, 44. /*Ivy Images:* Norman Lightfoot, 11. /Fred Bruemmer, 12, 20, 29, 33, 38-39, 43. /*Thomas Stack & Associates:* Randy Morse, 15. /*Eco-Art Productions:* Norman Lightfoot, 19. /Wayne Lynch, 23.